Perfect
WILTSHIRE

MARK BAUER

HALSGROVE

First published in Great Britain in 2010

Copyright © Mark Bauer 2010

British Library Cataloguing-in-Publication Data
A CIP record for this title is available from the British Library

ISBN 978 1 84114 998 1

HALSGROVE
Halsgrove House,
Ryelands Industrial Estate,
Bagley Road, Wellington, Somerset TA21 9PZ
Tel: 01823 653777   Fax: 01823 216796
email: sales@halsgrove.com

Part of the Halsgrove group of companies.
Information on all Halsgrove titles is available at: www.halsgrove.com

Printed and bound in China by Toppan Leefung Printing Ltd

ACKNOWLEDGEMENTS

Many people have helped me during the making of this book and I would like to say a few thank yous. Firstly, to mum, who lives in Berkshire, but conveniently near the Wiltshire border, and let me treat her house like a hotel whilst I was exploring and taking photographs of the north and east of the county. Also to my partner Julie and our son Harry, who put up (almost!) uncomplainingly with my disappearing at unearthly hours and often not returning until several days later.

Tony Blake was a constant source of help and encouragement throughout this project, and his brother Andrew took time out from his busy schedule to give me an invaluable tour of Wiltshire when I first started work on the book.

Finally, during my travels through Wiltshire I met numerous locals who were only too willing to share viewpoints and subject matter. I now know why they were so proud of their county.

DEDICATION

For Mum

INTRODUCTION

It has struck me that, apart from the more obvious locations such as Stonehenge and Salisbury Cathedral, Wiltshire is an underphotographed county. When taking the photographs for this book, I frequently had the landscape to myself – something that would be a rare treat in Dorset, where I carry out a lot of my work.

This is certainly not to suggest that Wiltshire is lacking in interest. Far from it – it has more prehistoric sites than any other county, including in Avebury and Stonehenge, two of the most important in Europe. Just around the corner from Avebury is the enigmatic Silbury Hill – the largest man-made mound in Europe – whose purpose, despite extensive research, remains a mystery. There is also the Ridgeway, arguably Britain's oldest road, and a number of chalk carvings – again, more than any other county. There is plenty of less obvious history too, in the form of numerous Iron Age hill forts, and ancient tracts of woodland such as Savernake Forest.

There is beautiful and quintessentially English landscape, too, from the rolling hills of Cranborne Chase in the south, to the edge of the Cotswold Area of Outstanding Natural Beauty in the north. The county has more than its fair share of historic buildings – Old Wardour Castle and Malmesbury Abbey being my personal favourites – and some charming villages, including Castle Combe, surely one of the prettiest in England.

Living by the sea in Dorset, water plays a large part in my photography, and I must confess that at the start of this project, the prospect of photographing a landlocked county was somewhat daunting. I needn't have worried however, as I came across plenty of inspirational locations: from the magnificent Lake Shear Water near Longleat, to the quiet, unassuming beauty of the chalk streams flowing through Salisbury Plain.

People are always interested in the equipment I use, so here it is. Until fairly recently, I was shooting mostly with 6x7cm transparency film, but this book was shot entirely with digital equipment – the first time I've used digital exclusively for a major project. I used a Canon 1ds mark II and a Canon 5D mark II. My two most used lenses were the 17-40mm wide angle zoom, and the 24-105mm zoom. Although working digitally now, I still prefer in-camera filtration to spending hours in front of the computer, and commonly use neutral density graduated filters to tone down bright skies, and a polarising filter to reduce glare and increase colour saturation. I also occasionally use 'solid' neutral density filters to enable me to use long exposures and capture a sense of movement.

The majority of the photographs in this book were taken at the very beginning or end of the day – the 'golden hours' for photography, when the light is magical, and the strong hues and colours need no help from computer manipulation.

Finally, I have a confession to make. Although I grew up near the Berkshire–Wiltshire border, before I started work on this book, I didn't really know Wiltshire very well. It can take many years to truly get to know a county, and I hope that in the 18 months I had to produce the images for this book, I have been able to do it justice. It's certainly a county I will continue to visit and photograph.

Mark Bauer

January 2010

The rolling hills of the West Wiltshire Downs are shrouded in mist at daybreak in late summer.

Winter sunset, looking towards Shaftesbury in Dorset, from Win Green Hill.

The mist in the valleys of the West Wiltshire Downs creates a beautiful layering effect.

Winter sunrise over Cranborne Chase.

Opposite:
The Ox Drove, Win Green Hill, on a frosty January morning. This ancient track
divides the picture into two halves – one warm, one cold.

Above:
The beech clump on top of Win Green Hill
is a well-known local landmark.

Right:
A misty dawn at Cranborne Chase. The chalk plateau
covers around 380 square miles, straddling Wiltshire,
Hampshire and Dorset, and has been designated
an Area of Outstanding Natural Beauty.

The first day of spring,
Cranborne Chase.

The beech clump on top of Win Green Hill is just
visible across the rolling hills of Cranborne Chase.

An atmospheric early
spring sunrise near the
border with Dorset.

The Palladian bridge and lake at Stourhead. The gardens at Stourhead, now managed by the National Trust, are some of the finest eighteenth-century gardens in the country.

Tulip tree, Stourhead lake.

The autumn colours at Stourhead are set off against the backdrop of a stormy sky.

King Alfred's Tower, near Stourhead. This imposing folly was built by Henry Hoare to commemorate the end of the Seven Years' War against France, and was completed in 1772.

Low clouds drift over a hill near Norton Ferris.

Storm clouds racing over Pepperbox Hill, south east of Salisbury.

Salisbury Cathedral from across the Harnham Water Meadows,
during the 'Big Freeze' in the winter of 2008/2009.

Salisbury Cathedral from the Town Path Bridge in Queen Elizabeth Gardens.

25

The Ebble at Odstock, swollen by heavy winter rain.

Looking across the moat to Old Sarum. It began life as an Iron Age hill fort and by the middle ages had developed into a town. The population eventually outgrew it and the town of New Sarum – now the city of Salisbury – was founded.

27

Remains inside Old Sarum.

Late afternoon light in winter, near Imber Range on Salisbury Plain. Around 150 square miles of Salisbury Plain are owned by the MOD, and are used as a training area. With agricultural development being prevented, much of the Plain has become a haven for some rare species of flora and fauna.

A stormy winter sky over the hills of Salisbury Plain, just outside Tilshead.

Winter sunrise near Tilshead.

A barn breaks up the open landscape of Salisbury Plain near Orcheston.

The imposing All Saints' church at Chitterne.

Regimental badges were first carved into the hillside of Fovant Down during the First World War.

The River Ebble on
a frosty morning.

Above:
The interior of St Martin of Tours, Fifield Bavant.

Opposite:
The thirteenth-century church of St Martin of Tours at Fifield Bavant
is the smallest parish church in Wiltshire, and still in regular use.

The Ebble as it flows past Fifield Bavant.

Opposite:
Sunset over Fonthill Lake, Fonthill Bishop, near Tisbury. The lake was
used for the filming of the river scenes in the film *Chocolat*.

Another connection with the silver screen – Old Wardour Castle
was featured in the 1991 film, *Robin Hood: Prince of Thieves.*

Now managed by English Heritage, Old Wardour Castle is one of the hidden gems of Wiltshire – a ruin, but an extremely romantic one.

41

Another detail from the castle.

Tucked away in the Nadder Valley is the almost perfectly preserved village
of Teffont Evias. The church in particular has a wonderful setting.

Above:
A closer view of the church.

Right:
Wiltshire's most famous monument under a soft sky at dawn.

One of the most important prehistoric sites in Europe,
if not the world, Stonehenge is an impressive sight.

A quintessential English village, Sherrington
is in an ideal spot next to a large duckpond.

Poppies near the village of Codford.

A spectacular poppy field near the village of Hanging Langford.

Above:
A closer view of the Hanging Langford poppies.

Right:
Just down the road, at Steeple Langford, is Langford Lakes
Nature Reserve, managed by Wiltshire Wildlife Trust.

A still winter sunrise
at Langford Lakes.

The last of the autumn leaves cling stubbornly to the branches
of the trees lining the River Wylie near Great Wishford.

Another view of the Wylie, in late autumn.

Larmer Tree Gardens, created in 1880 by General Pitt Rivers. The Larmer Tree was the original border between Dorset and Wiltshire.

Above:
There is an excellent collection of trees at Larmer Tree Gardens.

Opposite:
The Church of St Peter and St Paul, at Longbridge Deverill enjoys
a lovely setting on a gentle slope above the River Deverill.

The Deverill at
Longbridge Deverill.

The view west from Little Knoll, near Maiden Bradley, on a summer's evening.

A balloonist makes the most of a still summer evening near Maiden Bradley.

59

Early morning mist lying in the valley near Mere.

White Sheet Hill on a summer afternoon.

There are fabulous views over the Longleat estate from Heaven's Gate.

Steam rises from the trees at Lake Shear Water after
a heavy shower at the end of a summer's day.

The sun breaks through heavy clouds at Lake Shear Water at sunset.

The substantial Iron Age hill fort of Cley Hill, near Warminster.

Looking south from Cley Hill.

Autumn colours at Roundway Hill near Devizes.

The low autumn sun brings out the folds of the hills at Roundway Down.

Roundway Down was the site of a major battle in
the Civil War, and a victory for the Royalists.

Opposite:
Beech tress in autumn sunshine at Roundway Hill.

Sunset clouds gusting over Roundway Hill.

Poppies on the banks
of the Kennet and
Avon Canal at
Caen Hill Locks
near Devizes.

There is a total of 29 locks at Caen Hill, rising 237 feet in 2 miles. This is the bottom of the main flight of 16 locks.

Barges at the top of the locks.

Herons are a common sight on the banks of the locks.

Cherhill Down, showing the white horse
and the Lansdowne monument.

The Cherhill white horse. Cut in 1780, it is the
second oldest of the Wiltshire white horses.

The Lansdowne monument stands near the white horse at the top of Cherhill Down.
It was erected by Sir William Petty in 1845 and purportedly stands on a ley line.

View from the top of Cherhill Down.

On top of Cherhill Down is the hill fort of Oldbury Castle, which is said to be haunted by the ghosts of Roman soldiers.

Haunted or not, there are certainly spectacular views from the hill fort.

The church at Bishops Cannings, rising through the mist on a December morning.

Winter mist diffuses the rising sun over Bishops Cannings.

Opposite:
Cloudscape over fields near Etchilhampton.

The oldest of the white horses, at Westbury.

The Bath stone of Bradford-on-Avon, glowing in the early morning sun.

Castle Combe is probably the best known of the Wiltshire villages, and deservedly so –
it is a classic English village and has been used as a film location for various period dramas.

St Andrew's church,
Castle Combe.

Easton Grey is a pretty village of Cotswold stone on the River Avon.

There is a fine Georgian manor house just outside the village.

The church at West Kington has a commanding position on top of a hill.

A clearing shower over Kington St Michael.

Malmesbury Abbey. The present building dates from the twelfth century,
but there has been a monastery on the site since around 676.

Malmesbury Abbey viewed from across the Avon.

Dawn at Mallard Lake which is the largest of the lakes in Lower Moor Farm Nature Reserve, in the Cotswold Water Park and has been designated a Site of Special Scientific Interest.

The sun rising through the trees at Mallard Lake.

Formed from the flooding of old gravel pits, the lakes are important wildlife habitats.

Cottage Lake, one of the two smaller lakes at Lower Moor Farm, on a late autumn morning.

The Alton Barnes white horse, hidden in the snow.

Opposite
. . . And revealed more clearly, on a summer's evening.

A frosty dawn at the Cove, Avebury. Avebury is perhaps less well-known than Stonehenge, but is older, and one of the largest Neolithic monuments in Europe. Being able to walk freely among the stones makes visiting the site a special experience.

Opposite
Avebury stones glowing in the first light of the day.

A snowy scene at the Cove in Avebury.

A mackerel sky over Avebury stones.

The West Kennet Avenue, which links Avebury and The Sanctuary on Overton Hill.

Opposite:
Dawn landscape near Avebury.

The enigmatic Silbury Hill,
a man-made hill, the first
phase of which was built in
about 2700BC. Although
research has managed to
discover when and how it
was constructed, why
remains a mystery.

The River Kennet near Avebury, on a frosty morning.

Silbury Hill, viewed
from across the
Kennet.

A dawn sky over West Overton.

A stormy sky adds a sense of drama to Barbury Castle,
an Iron Age hill fort which lies on the Ridgeway.

Dappled light on the fields below Barbury Castle.

Passing storm clouds over a beech clump on the Ridgeway
National Trail. The Ridgeway is arguably Europe's oldest road.

Looking west from the Ridgeway near Winterbourne Monkton.

Opposite:
The hills flanking the Ridgeway look harsh in winter frost.

Sunset clouds drift over the white horse at Hackpen Hill.

A beech clump on the Ridgeway, under a pink cloud at sunset.

Winter trees silhouetted by the setting sun near Hackpen Hill.

The Kennet and Avon Canal frozen over during the 'Big Freeze' in 2009.

Snow lining the banks of
the Kennet and Avon just
outside Great Bedwyn.

A tranquil canal scene
near Great Bedwyn.

123

The windmill at Wilton, near Marlborough, is Wiltshire's only operating windmill. It was built in 1821 to replace the watermills which were no longer able to operate after the Kennet and Avon Canal had taken water from the River Bedwyn.

The windmill is a very distinctive sight at dusk.

Autumn colours in Savernake
Forest near Marlborough.

Savernake is one of the great forests of
England – older than the New Forest –
and was a royal hunting preserve. Henry
VIII is supposed to have met Jane
Seymour after hunting in the forest.

The forest has a very different atmosphere in winter fog.

Twilight clouds over
Pewsey Downs.

Heavy clouds threaten
further snowfall over
Pewsey Downs.

Left:
A peaceful early
morning scene at
Pewsey Wharf.

Right:
A sunny afternoon,
just outside
Marlborough.

Bluebells carpet the forest floor at West Woods, near Marlborough.

West Woods consists almost entirely of beech trees. The bluebells make it a popular spot with visitors in May.

A light summer mist hangs over the hills in this view from Oare Hill.

A wintry view over the Vale of Pewsey, from Martinsell Hill.

Winter sunset over
Martinsell Hill.

The Iron Age hill fort at Martinsell is quite substantial, covering 32 acres. It is also a wonderfully atmospheric place to spend some time.

A lone tree on Martinsell, set against the snowy backdrop of the Pewsey Vale.